What I Have Learned from
BEING A TEACHER

What I Have Learned from
BEING A TEACHER

DR. PATRICIA POWELL JOHNSON

What I Have Learned From Being a Teacher

Copyright © 2021 by Dr. Patricia Powell Johnson. All rights reserved.

No part of this publication may be reproduced, stored in a retrieval system or transmitted in any way by any means, electronic, mechanical, photocopy, recording or otherwise without the prior permission of the author except as provided by USA copyright law.

The opinions expressed by the author are not necessarily those of URLink Print and Media.

1603 Capitol Ave., Suite 310 Cheyenne, Wyoming USA 82001
1-888-980-6523 | admin@urlinkpublishing.com

URLink Print and Media is committed to excellence in the publishing industry.

Book design copyright © 2021 by URLink Print and Media. All rights reserved.

Published in the United States of America

Library of Congress Control Number: 2021916859
ISBN 978-1-64753-925-2 (Paperback)
ISBN 978-1-64753-926-9 (Digital)

03.06.21

Introduction

After being a teacher, lecturer, administrator, instructor, associate professor, consultant, and a dedicated, empathetic educator for the past 45 years, and after working in a variety of classrooms at every level, PK-16+, and after teaching a variety of content areas, I have learned a lot about life, people, education, and myself. This book presents a synopsis of some of the things I have learned. The idea came to me through the inspiration from the Holy Spirit and I woke up in the middle of the night and just started writing all the things that were on my mind. God's goodness and grace have allowed me to travel to many diverse places, to interact with experts at all levels of education and to work in all kinds of educational settings from pre-school classrooms to university administration. The knowledge I now possess has come to me from a variety of sources, including all types of literature, Bible study, personal experiences, research-based best practices, professionals I have either worked with or met along the way, my interactions with family, friends, students, and parents, both young and old, and my voracious love for children, for teaching, for books, reading, and increasing knowledge.

Dedication

This book is dedicated to my children, Shun, Dee, Karl, Tamara, Brittainee, my godchildren, grandchildren, my adopted family, my foster family, and my husband, Rickey, for their unconditional support and love for me. Their patience with me, faith in me, encouraging words to me, and willingness to "drive Mrs. Daisy" will forever have an impact on my life and my work.

Acknowledgements

I would like to acknowledge my friend Wilma, who has always believed in my potential to write a good book. I want to thank my friend, Dr. Paul Cooks whose prolific writing inspires me to do more, and my colleague Dr. Tyrone Burton, who ignited the spark in me to continue my writing. I want to also acknowledge my mentor, Augusta, my friend, Barbara and my co-workers, Melanie, Rosiland, and Tiffany, who support me in everything that I do. Finally, I want to acknowledge my Father in Heaven who gives me wisdom, love, forgiveness, mercy, strength, and inspiration on a daily basis.

Table of Contents

Introduction 5
Dedication 7
Acknowledgements 9
What I Have Learned About Children 13
What I Have Learned About Parents and Guardians 14
What I Have Learned About Education 15
What I Have Learned About Educators 16
What I Have Learned About Schools 17
What I Have Learned About Communities 18
What I Have Learned About Religious Beliefs 19
What I Have Learned About What Children Value 20
What I Have Learned About What Parents Value 21
What I Have Learned About What Teachers Value 22
What I Have Learned About What School Administrators Value 23
What I Have Learned About What Politicians Value 24
What I Have Learned About Time 25
What I Have Learned About Love 26
What I Have Learned About Money 27
What I Have Learned About Fashion 28
What I Have Learned About Health and Wellness 29
What I Have Learned About Stress 30
What I Have Learned About Listening 31
What I Have Learned About Reading 32
What I Have Learned About Teaching and Learning 33
What I Have Learned About Expectations 34
What I Have Learned About Excuses 35
What I Have Learned About Resourcefulness 36

What I Have Learned About Duty and Responsibility 37
What I Have Learned About Planning 38
What I Have Learned About Assessment....................................39
What I Have Learned About Differentiating Instruction............ 40
What I Have Learned About What Really Matters 41
What I Have Learned About Silence... 42
What I Have Learned About Cooperative Learning..................... 43
What I Have Learned About Effective Classroom Management...... 44
What I Have Learned About Taking Risks...................................45
What I Have Learned About Initiative... 46
What I Have Learned About Intelligence 47
What I Have Learned About Prayer.. 48
What I Have Learned About Winning and Losing...................... 49
What I Have Learned About Grades... 50
What I Have Learned About Self-Esteem.....................................51
What I Have Learned About Numbers 52
What I Have Learned About Procrastination...............................53
What I Have Learned About Life 54
What I Have Learned About People (Young and Old)..................56
What I Have Learned About Living Well.....................................57

What I Have Learned About Children

Children…
 …are our most valuable assets.
 …can and do learn.
All children need support.
All children are important.
Some children may need interventions.
All children can teach us something.
All children are good at something.
All children have potential.
Some children may need behavior contracts.
All children deserve love and respect.
All children want to feel worthy, wanted, and welcome.
All children need another chance.
Some children may need remediation.
All children can be good.
All children are STAR students.
All children are at risk.
God views children as especially important.
"Children are likely to live up to what you believe of them." Lady Bird Johnson
"Children must be taught how to think, not what to think." Margaret Mead
"Children are not things to be molded, but people to be unfolded." Jess Lair

What I Have Learned About Parents and Guardians

All parents…
- …want their children to succeed.
- …want to help you with their children.
- …care about their children.
- …care about teaching and learning.
- …are the child's first teacher.
- …have beliefs and values.
- …have unique parenting styles and skills.
- …are interested in their children.
- …need confidence and support.
- …need clear guidelines and expectations for success.
- …need to feel safe and secure.
- …need to feel accepted and loved.
- …need to feel a sense of accomplishment.

All parents have some degree of income, interests, ideas, investment, irritation, and interaction with education, with teachers, and with children.

"One of the greatest titles in the world is parent, and one of the biggest blessings in the world is to have parents to call mom and dad." Jim DeMint

"We may not be able to prepare the future for our children, but we can at least prepare our children for the future." Franklin D. Roosevelt

What I Have Learned About Education

Education...
- ...is important.
- ...is necessary.
- ...is enabling.
- ...should be free and appropriate.
- ...should leave no child behind.
- ...is often complex.
- ...is often politically motivated.
- ...is constantly changing.
- ...is constantly moving.
- ...is not an option, it is a must and a civil right.
- ...is not "one size fits all".
- ...should be inclusive.
- ...is not always fair.
- ...is not always equal.
- ...is not always easy.
- ...is not sufficiently funded.
- ...is the key.

Education makes a difference in people and in circumstances.

Education opens doors.

Education is a precursor for success.

What I Have Learned About Educators

Educators…
- …are everywhere.
- …are enablers.
- …are different.
- …are censored.
- …are unique.
- …are special.
- …are leaders.
- …are counselors.
- …are advocates.
- …are caregivers.
- …are sometimes handicapped.
- …are often political.
- …are often angels in disguise.
- …are not always unified.
- …are not always valued.
- …need a model.
- …need a back-up plan.
- …often need a "bag of tricks."
- …are parents and guardians.
- …are smart, serious, sane, sensible, and sensitive.

What I Have Learned About Schools

Schools are…
- …Learning Communities.
- …Political.
- …Symbolic.
- …Resourceful.
- …Challenged.
- …Competitive.
- …Constantly Changing.
- …Interactive.
- …Innovative.
- …Inclusive.
- …Goal Oriented.
- …Visionary.
- …Safe Havens.
- …Purpose Driven.
- …Laboratories.
- …Financial Institutions.
- …Mental Institutions.
- …Valued and Valuable.
- …Academically and Socially Under resourced.
- …Sometimes Dysfunctional.

What I Have Learned About Communities

Communities are...

    ...valued and valuable.

    ...influential.

    ...racially, economically, religiously, and socially diverse.

    ...historical.

    ...social units with common norms, customs, values or identity.

    ...both small and large.

    ...vitally important to the growth and success of the members.

Communities...

    ...share a sense of place situated in a particular geographic area.

    ...are made up of people with similar values.

    ...can be urban, suburban, or rural.

    ...are stronger together.

    ...support members.

    ...promote open, participative development,

    ...allow members to share a sense of personal relatedness.

    ...can be joined by interests, actions, place, or practice.

    ...cooperate to make improvements.

    ...work toward common goals.

    ...depend on equitable funding.

    ...celebrate differences.

    ...provide a sense of belonging and pride.

A community is a safe, cohesive, confident, prosperous and happy place.

What I Have Learned About Religious Beliefs

Religious Beliefs are…

…important.
…individual.
…attitudes and practice.
…faith-based.
…life changing.
…to be recognized and accepted.
…to be acknowledged.
…to be respected and valued.
…to be explored.
…to be expressed.

Religious beliefs can…

…change.
…change people and situations.
…be insightful.
…be as different as the people who hold them.
…set the stage for building relationships.
…set the stage for interactions with others.
…be shaped by life experiences.
…influence one's well-being.
…be motivational.
…be fluid.
…be static.

Church is not mandatory. It's voluntary and operates mostly with volunteers.

What I Have Learned About What Children Value

Children value...
    ...their parents' opinion.
    ...their siblings.
    ...their friends.
    ...their sense of safety.
    ...their sense of belonging.
    ...their sense of self-worth.
    ...their knowledge.
    ...their ability to grasp new concepts.
    ...their own ideas and beliefs.
    ...their own success.
    ...their sense of pride.
    ...feeling wanted and loved.
    ...feeling respected.
    ...feeling accepted for who they are.
    ...something they can claim as their own.
    ...growing up.
    ...making progress.
    ...making new friends.
    ...making an impression on others.
    ...good examples.

Children don't care how much you know until they know how much you care.

What I Have Learned About What Parents Value

Parents value...

...their support groups.
...their knowledge.
...their past experiences.
...their homes.
...their families.
...their reputation.
...their religion.
...their lifestyles.
...their church affiliation.
...their sense of accomplishment.
...their sense of self-worth.
...work that is rewarding and satisfying.
...their own safety and their children's safety.
...their children's success.
...their faith.
...their sense of belonging.
...other people's opinions of them.
...their worth in the community.
...the things they own.
...help from others.
...their own success.
...their peace of mind.

What I Have Learned About What Teachers Value

Teachers value...

    ...research-based best practices.
    ...their own education.
    ...inclusion.
    ...praise and recognition for hard work.
    ...their own leadership styles.
    ...their own success inside and outside of the classroom.
    ...their place in society.
    ...their autonomy.
    ...their work and careers.
    ...their students.
    ...their own children.
    ...their coworkers.
    ...their peers.
    ...their faith.
    ...their personal and professional relationships.
    ...their potential for greater.
    ...their understanding of differences.
    ...their understanding of special needs.
    ...their own reputation.
    ...monetary compensation for work well done.

What I Have Learned About What School Administrators Value

School Administrators value...
- ...research-based best practices.
- ...their position.
- ...their prestige.
- ...their power.
- ...their vision.
- ...their potential for greater.
- ...their educational achievements.
- ...their relationships with others.
- ...their influence.
- ...their ability to communicate.
- ...their leadership styles and skills.
- ...their persuasiveness.
- ...their students.
- ...their families.
- ...parents, and other stakeholders.
- ...their peers.
- ...their coworkers.
- ...their productivity.
- ...their professionalism.
- ...their performance.
- ...their ability to transform.

What I Have Learned About What Politicians Value

Politicians value their...
- ...politics.
- ...position.
- ...place in society.
- ...power.
- ...reputation.
- ...success.
- ...laws and policies.
- ...political influence.
- ...ability to raise funds.
- ...relationships.
- ...families.
- ...constituents' opinion.
- ...possessions.
- ...passion for causes.
- ...support from community.
- ...personal accomplishments.
- ...lifestyle.
- ...political achievements.
- ...image.
- ...future.

What I Have Learned About Time

Time is…
  …fleeting.
  …fluid.
  …money.
  …valuable.
  …once lost, gone.
  …to be treasured.
  …to be used wisely.
  …to be respected.
  …worthy of protection.
  …opportunity.
  …to be managed judiciously.
  …precious.
  …limited.
  …waits for no one.

Everyone is given the same amount of time.
Time can make the difference.
You should always respect other people's time.
Save time by being prepared.
Expect the unexpected.

What I Have Learned About Love

Love...
 ...begins with self.
 ...should be freely given.
 ...is to be shared.
 ...is to be demonstrated.
 ...should be voiced in words.
 ...should be demonstrated in actions.
 ...can be good to you and good for you.
 ...can be stifling to some.
 ...can be awesome.
 ...will make you do right.
 ...will make you do wrong.
 ...is reciprocal.
 ...is free, but expensive.
 ...is worth it.
 ...is inclusive.
 ...changes.
 ...stays the same.
 ...forgives.
 ...is patient.
 ...is longsuffering.
 ...is real.

What I Have Learned About Money

Money...
 ...is hard-earned and easily-spent.
 ...is symbolic of position, prestige, and power.
 ...cannot buy love.
 ...is often equated with success.
 ...does not make the person.
 ...can be wasted.
 ...is a commodity.
 ...is used to buy goods and services.
 ...is used to pay debts.
 ...cannot buy happiness.
 ...can be used wisely.
 ...sometimes affects a person's sense of self-worth.
 ...may affect a person's self-esteem.
 ... should not determine one's self-worth.
 ...can be a source of happiness.
 ...can be a source of grief.
 ...can be an influence for good.
 ...can be an influence for evil.
 ...is not a substitute for love.
 ...cannot buy common sense.

What I Have Learned About Fashion

Fashion...
- ...is just a statement.
- ...is temporary in nature.
- ...depends on the person wearing it.
- ...changes.
- ...comes and goes.
- ...is not equivalent to popularity.
- ...can transform an image.
- ...can depend on the current trends.
- ...is not always fashionable.
- ...can make a positive or a negative statement.
- ...provides clues to your character.
- ...provides clues to your personality.
- ...can mask true feelings.
- ...tells a story.
- ...has an agenda.
- ...can be competitive.
- ...highlights a person's features, good and bad.
- ..."one size does not fit all".

What I Have Learned About Health and Wellness

Health and Wellness...
- ... are interrelated.
- ...are different.
- ...are important.
- ... can affect productivity.
- ... can improve your life.
- ... affect your energy level.
- ... affect your performance.
- ... affect your emotions.
- ... require commitment.
- ... are critical for life alignment.
- ... require a balanced diet.
- ... require consistent exercise.
- ... are impacted by smoking habits.
- ...are impacted by drinking habits.
- ...are impacted by sleeping habits.
- ...improve with regular routines.
- ...require you to set goals.
- ...require you to monitor your progress.

"Take care of yourself so you can take care of your business."

What I Have Learned About Stress

Stress…
- … limits productivity.
- …creates more stress.
- …can lead to other health and wellness issues.
- …can be challenging.
- …can be good or bad.
- …can test your patience.
- …can affect your mood.
- …can affect your performance.
- …can affect your relationships.
- …affects people differently.
- …has a correlation to authority and position.
- …has lots of variables.
- …impacts your interactions with others.
- …can create emotional and physical tension.
- …can create anxiety and depression.
- …can create anger, anxiety, and irritability.
- …can be overwhelming.
- …can be monitored and controlled.
- …anyone can experience stress at any time.

What I Have Learned About Listening

Listening…
- …allows for a better understanding.
- …influences responses.
- …helps improve communication.
- …helps avoid danger.
- …is often better than talking.
- …promotes positive relationships.
- …encourages trust.
- …takes time and patience.
- …is a sign of caring.
- …improves clarity.
- …involves complex affective, behavioral, and cognitive processes.
- …can reveal amazing results.
- …contributes to overall success.
- …is hard work.
- …models professionalism.
- …shows respect for self and others.
- …eliminates too much pride.
- …creates opportunities.
- …involves paying attention.

"Most people do not listen with the intent to understand; they listen with the intent to reply." Stephen Covey

What I Have Learned About Reading

Reading...
...is fundamental.
...is fun.
...is a key to success.
...must be developmentally appropriate.
...requires pre-reading skills.
...opens doors.
...deepens knowledge.
...improves understanding.
...engages your mind.
...increases your vocabulary.
...allows you to travel vicariously.
...opens your mind to possibilities.
...increases your "quality of life" experiences.
...provides momentum.
...allows for personal and professional growth.
...expands your horizons.
...increases your knowledge base.
...helps you to help others.
...involves the use of context clues.

...reduces the gap between vocabulary, understanding, and expression.

Children learn to read by hearing others read and by reading themselves.

What I Have Learned About Teaching and Learning

Teaching and Learning…
- …create opportunities for new learning.
- …give you a sense of accomplishment.
- …open doors to communication.
- …allow you to help others.
- …broaden your horizons.
- …create a sense of community.
- …promote education.
- …should leave no child behind.
- …empower the teacher and the learner.
- …help you grow professionally.
- …create opportunities for success.
- …build relationships.
- …produce results.
- …are rewarding and satisfying.
- …are critical to our communities and our nation.
- …make us strive for better.
- …help us to breach the unknown
- …help us to embrace change.
- …help us to reduce stress.
- …help us to become better and to look for greater.

Teaching helps to facilitate Learning.
Teaching involves planning, design, standards, content, selection, directing, modeling, delivery, assessment and reflection.

What I Have Learned About Expectations

Expectations…
- …are important.
- …should be set high, but attainable.
- …can influence performance.
- …can influence behavior.
- …set boundaries.
- …allow for "freedom within limits".
- …increase productivity.
- …offer motivation.
- …help us reach our goals.
- …lead to consistency.
- …set "norms".
- …get results.
- …can reduce uncertainty and disappointment.
- …can transform people.
- …can transform situations.
- …improve management.
- …improve organization.
- …improve discipline.
- …are indicators of effective leadership.
- …lead to greater achievement.
- …create more potential.
- …create more success.

What I Have Learned About Excuses

Excuses…
- …do not excuse you or your actions.
- …often don't change the situation.
- …run out.
- …affect your credibility.
- …limit productivity.
- …avoid responsibility.
- …increase inconsistency.
- …can be exhausting.
- …can be limiting.
- …do not result in positive change.
- …can lead to poverty.
- …can lead to loss.
- …can create negative momentum.
- …can lead to destructive behavior.
- …can be interpreted as laziness.
- …are an inconvenience.
- …are a waste of time and effort.
- …increase stress levels.
- …impact your reputation.

Give people a reason and a solution, not an excuse!
Be honest with yourself about what you can do better!

What I Have Learned About Resourcefulness

Resourcefulness...
　　...gets results.
　　...meets needs.
　　...creates opportunities.
　　...saves time and money.
　　...increases preparedness.
　　...increases success rates.
　　...increases access.
　　...reduces inferiority.
　　...reduces deprivation.
　　...supports equity.
　　...supports equality.
　　...increases achievement.
　　...establishes options.
　　...increases economic opportunities.
　　...increases productivity.
　　...increases efficiency.
　　...increases effectiveness.
　　...recognizes potential.
　　...recognizes value.
　　...celebrates efforts.
　　...increases motivation.
　　...helps you find a way to achieve your goals.
　　...helps you to seek alternatives.

What I Have Learned About Duty and Responsibility

Duty and Responsibility…
- …improve success rates.
- …increase productivity.
- …are to be fulfilled and not evaded.
- …recognize individual differences.
- …reduce violations.
- …eliminate mistakes.
- …improve problem-solving.
- …establish expectations.
- …increase accountability.
- …establish foundations.
- …reduce stress levels.
- …reduce anxiety.
- …won't allow you to be a quitter.
- …allow for accommodations.
- …allow for adjustments.
- …save time.
- …save money.
- …improve performance.
- …impact versatility.
- …impact marketability.

Do what you have to do first, then you can do what you want to do.

Never, ever give up!

What I Have Learned About Planning

Planning...
    ...is important.
    ...is critical to success.
    ...reduces stress.
    ...limits chances of failure.
    ...provides the "road map".
    ...should be inclusive.
    ...should be done in advance.
    ...should include interventions and remedial activities.
    ...increases accomplishments.
    ...increases productivity.
    ...reduces gaps and deficits.
    ...manifests more and better.
    ...impacts marketability.
    ...should be inclusive.
    ...gives you an advantage.
    ...opens doors for greater.
    ...builds relationships.
    ...improves results.

"It's better to "overplan" that to "underplan".
"Lack of planning on your part does not create an emergency on my part."
"Proper planning prevents poor performance."
"If you fail to plan, you plan to fail."
"Prior Planning Saves Time. Poor Planning Wastes Time."

What I Have Learned About Assessment

Assessment…
- …is important.
- …is not always a pencil and paper test.
- …needs to be frequent.
- …should match objectives.
- …should be made clear prior to instruction.
- …should occur in the least restrictive environment.
- …should be valid.
- …should be reliable.
- …should be inclusive.
- …should document learning.
- …should be differentiated.
- …should prompt improvement in teaching and learning.

- Test what you Teach!
- Inspect what you Expect!
- Check for Understanding Frequently and in a Variety of Ways
- Practice Before You Test!
- Plan for Assessment when you Plan for Instruction.
- Match Objectives, Activities, Materials, and Assessments.
- There are many different ways to find out what students know and can do.
- Conduct Informal, Intermittent, and Formal Assessments.
- If at first you don't succeed, try, try again.

What I Have Learned About Differentiating Instruction

Differentiating Instruction...
    ...addresses content, process, and product.
    ...enables all students to learn at higher levels.
    ...recognizes individual differences in students.
    ...accommodates different learning styles.
    ...increases higher order thinking skills (HOTS)
    ...acknowledges multiple intelligences.
    ...recognizes that there is more than one way to be smart.
    ...employs cooperative learning strategies.
    ...can lead to more creative thinking.
    ...addresses students' readiness, interests and abilities.
    ...improves performance for all students.
    ...should include remedial and enrichment activities.
    ...accommodates learning styles.
    ...allows for effective time management.
    ...helps with effective classroom management.
    ...reduces discipline problems.
    ...creates community.
    ...improves teaching and learning.
    ...offers challenges for teachers and students.
    ...allows for self-reflection.
    ...allows for professional growth.
    ...creates opportunities for success.

What I Have Learned About What Really Matters

What Really Matters?
"Quality Trumps Quantity"
"Do More, Less"
"Teach Less, More"
"Respect Yourself"
"Acknowledge your Strengths"
"Say What You Mean and Mean What You Say"
"Establish Boundaries"
"State Expectations"
"Set Priorities"
"Write it Down"
"Speak Your Mind"
"Follow Your Instincts"
"Practice What You Preach"
"Make a Plan and Follow Your Plan"
"Be the Model"
"Show Me the Helicopter"
"Action Speaks Louder than Words"
"Measure Twice, Cut Once"
"Think Before You Speak"
"Forethought is Better than Hindsight"
"Always Be Your Authentic Self"
"Always Be Honest"
"Don't Sweat the Small Stuff"

What I Have Learned About Silence

Silence…
- …is golden.
- …is powerful.
- …is a learning opportunity.
- …speaks volumes.
- …improves listening.
- …increases understanding.
- …creates a positive atmosphere.
- …creates an inviting learning environment.
- …is an exception, and not the rule.
- …creates trust.
- …can boost your overall well-being.
- …builds relationships.
- …creates community.
- …improves performance.
- …increases comprehension.
- …can open doors and windows to new adventures.
- …wins friends.
- …influences people.
- …is always an option.
- …leaves room for change.
- …creates room for improvement.

"Listen to silence. It has so much to say!" Rumi

What I Have Learned About Cooperative Learning

Cooperative Learning...
    ...should be inclusive.
    ...builds community.
    ...builds teams.
    ...improves teamwork.
    ...improves relationships.
    ...increases knowledge.
    ...allows for communication.
    ...allows for movement.
    ...improves classroom management.
    ...helps with time management.
    ...increases understanding.
    ...develops partnerships.
    ...increases academic performance.
    ...improves higher order thinking skills (HOTS)
    ...generates academic revenue.
    ...acknowledges multiple intelligences.
    ...recognizes different learning styles.
    ...acknowledges individual differences.
    ...accommodates variety.
    ...includes 'real life' experiences.
    ...includes a plan for early finishers.
    ...accommodates change.
    ...accommodates varying group sizes.
    ...makes learning fun.

What I Have Learned About Effective Classroom Management

Effective Classroom Management…

  …is important.
  …should be consistent.
  …is critical for academic success.
  …supports teacher retention.
  …saves time and energy.
  …can ensure a smooth-running classroom.
  …can prevent teacher burn-out.

Make a Plan and Follow Your Plan.
Establish Routines and Procedures.
Give Clear, Precise Directions.
Say What You Mean and Mean What You Say.
Establish Rewards and Consequences.
Establish a Signal.
Teach Your Students How to Resolve Conflicts
Use Cooperative/Collaborative Learning
Discipline is NOT the same as Management.
Effective Classroom Management reduces Discipline Referrals.
PLAN Ahead (Prepare, Look and Listen, Anticipate, Notice)
"Catch Them Doing Something Right."
Praise Frequently, Criticize Sparingly.
Acknowledge Effort.
Celebrate Success.
Rest if you must, but don't quit.

What I Have Learned About Taking Risks

Taking Risks…
    …can help you achieve future goals.
    …builds confidence.
    …requires courage.
    …can improve your skills.
    …can lead to a better life.
    …builds resilience.
    …can sometimes be stressful.
    …can sometimes be harmful.
    …can test your limits.
    …can help you go beyond what you believed was possible.
    …can help you face the fear of uncertainty.

> There are some good risks and some bad risks.
> Know your limits when taking risks.
> Don't be afraid to get out of your comfort zone.
> Life is a journey, not a destiny.
> "You don't bounce back. You bounce forward."
> Success creates success.
> Playing it safe all the time yields few rewards.
> Always have a back-up plan.
> Know when to Quit.
> Accept Ownership of Your Mistakes.

What I Have Learned About Initiative

Initiative…
   …means doing the right things without being told.
   …means you keep going when things get tough.
   …means you take advantage of the opportunities presented.
   …helps you to solve problems.
   …can help you to resolve conflict.
   …can help you grow professionally.
   …means you know how to be resourceful.
   …means using your head wisely.
   …means having the drive to achieve success.
   …is the ability to assess and start things going independently.
   …is having the motivation and power to act or take charge.
   …means you know how to get things under control
   …means you know how to implement an alternate strategy,
   …is having a fresh, new approach to things.

Tough Times Never Last, but Tough People Do!
Pray Before You Leap!
Act, don't react!
Keep it Short and Simple (KISS)
Learn to Speak the King's English.
Improve the Situation When Necessary.

What I Have Learned About Intelligence

Intelligence…
 …is a trait that everyone possesses.
 …can be practical, creative, and analytical.
 …can be improved.
 …involves reasoning.
 …involves Higher Order Thinking Skills (HOTS)
 …is more than just "book learning".
 …is impacted by your life experiences.
 …can be affected by your social interactions.
 …can be manifested in a variety of ways.
 …can impact your ability to solve problems.
 …can be affected by your behavior.
 …is more than just a number.
 …impacts your creativity, critical thinking and problem-solving.
 …includes your capacity for logic.
 …involves your capacity for understanding.
 …can be manifested by your self-awareness.
 …can be impacted by your critical thinking skills.
 …can be impacted by your emotional state.
 …can affect your ability to learn at higher levels.
 …can be manifested by your creativity.
 …is sometimes compared to "street smarts".

What I Have Learned About Prayer

Prayer...

...keeps you humble.

...changes people.

...allows people to change things.

...includes A.C.T.S. (Adoration, Confession, Thanksgiving, Supplication)

...should be first done in private.

...is a two-way conversation with God.

...can be learned.

...should be uttered with an open heart.

...should be said with an open mind.

...can be intercessory.

...allows communication with God in thought, spoken or written words.

...is one of the most important things a Christian can do.

...does not have to be complicated.

...can be uttered by anyone.

...is powerful.

...can open blind eyes.

...can heal open wounds.

...can repair broken hearts.

...can fix broken lives.

> God has given us a Model Prayer.
> God hears and answers our prayers.
> We should pray for others.
> Jesus Taught His Disciples How to Pray.

What I Have Learned About Winning and Losing

Winning and Losing…
  Life is full of ups and downs. Enjoy the ride!
  Celebrate your wins.
  Learn from your failures.
  "We Fall Down, But We Get UP!"
  Effort Counts, too!
  Talk about your wins and your losses.
  Practice Good Sportsmanship.
  Show empathy to others when they lose.
  Acknowledge that losing is inevitable.
  Develop "True Grit".
  Learn to accept defeat.
  Don't get mad, get better!
  Practice Perseverance.
  Remember that "Life is Not Fair".
  You win some. You lose some.
  Joy is Contagious.
  Victory is to be celebrated.
  Strength comes from hardships and struggles.
  Failure is more important than victory.
  You will fail a lot more than you will win. Don't let it stop you.
  Capitalize on your losses.
  Losing teaches us crucial life lessons.
Your reactions to winning or losing can discourage or encourage you.

What I Have Learned About Grades

Grades...
- ...almost always count.
- ...communicate achievement.
- ...can be used for self-evaluation.
- ...sometimes determine future success in school and in life.
- ...are often used as criteria for college and careers.
- ...are one of many factors in determining success.
- ...can be impacted by your character.
- ...can be used as incentives.
- ...can become an obsession.
- ...are important based on your life goals.
- ...can grant access.
- ...can help you receive scholarships.
- ...can help you earn money for school.
- ...can help you gain entrance into certain organizations.
- ...should not be valued over knowledge.
- ...can sometimes make school seem stressful.
- ...come easy for some and not so easy for others.
- ...can build your confidence.
- ...can motivate you to do good work.
- ...can teach responsibility.
- ...should never be taken for granted.
- ...don't make the person.

What I Have Learned About Self-Esteem

Self-Esteem is...
...your own perception of your own self-worth.
...one of every individual's basic needs.
...impacted by your emotions.
...associated with your sense of pride and accomplishment.
...can be improved.
...associated with your personal values.
...associated with how well you like yourself.
...often subjective.
....how you feel about your limitations.
... your ability to focus on what you can change.
...one thing that affects your behavior.
...one thing that has an influence on your choices and decisions.
...one way you express your triumph, pride, and shame.
...impacted by the way you value yourself as a person.
...a manifestation of how much you appreciate yourself.
...how you feel about your appearance, abilities, and actions.
...a manifestation of your self-care.
...impacted by how well you explore your full potential.
...either high, low, or inflated.
...either healthy or unhealthy.

You are never too old to learn, grow, or change.

What I Have Learned About Numbers

Numbers...
    ...can help you count, measure and label.
    ...can be represented in digits or words.
    ...can be represented by symbols.
    ...can be memorized.
    ...are part of a mathematical system.
    ...can help you add, subtract, multiply and divide.
    ...can be used to order.
    ...can be used as codes.
    ...can form sets and subsets.
    ...can be expanded or extended.
    ...can be used to calculate.
    ...can be used in mathematical operations.
    ...have fundamental significance.
    ...have certain properties.
    ...have cultural significance.
    ...can help with problem-solving.
    ...can be simple or complex.
    ...can be applied to conventions.
    ...can be classified.
    ...can represent the amount in your bank account.
    ...can represent the page count of a book.
    ...can represent an approaching deadline.
    ...can be fascinating.

What I Have Learned About Procrastination

Procrastination…
- …happens when you put off doing what you should do.
- …can culminate in trouble.
- …can cause you to miss out on some things.
- …can impact your completion of important tasks.
- …often engages you in meaningless activities.
- …means intentionally putting things off until later.
- …can be a result of "perfectionism".
- …can create anxiety.
- …can result from feelings of guilt.
- …can affect your reputation.
- …can lead to disillusionment.
- …can lead to a need for remediation.
- …can wear you out.
- …can be impacted by attention deficit hyperactivity disorder.
- …can be impacted by bipolar disorder.
- …can be associated with depression.
- …can create higher levels of frustration.
- …can make you feel guilty.
- … can impact your self-esteem.
- …can lead to a need for some type of intervention.
- …seldom changes anything.
- …can impact your opportunities for success.

What I Have Learned About Life

Life…

"Life is Long." Aram Taghavi

"Life goes on."

"You only live once, but if you do it right, once is enough." Mae West

"The purpose of our lives is to be happy." Dalai Lama

"Get busy living or get busy dying." Stephen King

"Life is what happens when you are busy making other plans." John Lennon

"Small steps in the right direction can turn out to be the biggest step of your life." Good Housekeeping

"You can't go back and change the beginning, but you can start where you are and change the ending." C.S. Lewis

"The happiness of your life depends on the quality of your thoughts." Marcus Aurelius

"A life spent making mistakes is not only more honorable, but more useful than a life spent doing nothing." George Bernard Shaw

"Live for what's worth dying for, and leverage technology to create the world you wish to see." Aram Taghavi

"Love is necessary for a healthy life. Practice daily by loving everyone around you."

"Life really is simple, but we insist on making it complicated." Confucius

"Life is never made unbearable by circumstances, but only by lack of meaning and purpose." Viktor Frankl

"If you want happiness for an hour, take a nap. If you want happiness for a day, go fishing. If you want happiness for a year, inherit a fortune. If you want happiness for a lifetime, help someone else." Chinese Proverb

"Challenges are what make life interesting and overcoming the is what makes life meaningful." Joshua J. Marine

What I Have Learned About People (Young and Old)

People (young and old)...
...are mostly concerned about themselves.
...are mostly interested in their own hopes and dreams.
...want opportunities to talk about themselves.
...want you to ask them questions about themselves and their families.
...will lie.
...all have a story to tell.
...will show you what is important to them by how they live and how they treat other people.
...are often scared of something.
...can sometimes be rude.
...often have vulnerabilities that contribute to their fears.
...want to improve their lives and their circumstances.
...want to feel connected to others.
...often would rather hear your reasons instead of your excuses.
...often want to please others.
...want to win friends and influence other people.
...want to find humor in life.
...want to have hope for the future.
...sometimes really don't know the truth.
...want to believe in something or someone.
...are "autobiographical" in nature.
...believe that their perception is reality.
...are sometimes prideful.
...can be a source of strength.

What I Have Learned About Living Well

Living Well Means…
　…Taking Action.
　…Being Compassionate.
　…Having Determination.
　…Being Strong.
　…Being Mindful.
　…Loving Yourself and Loving Others.
　…Embracing a Healthy Mind, Body and Soul.
　…Creating Plans.
　…Focusing on Personal Growth.
　…Focusing on Professional Growth.
　…Celebrating Self-Discovery.
　…Knowing Your Power.
　…Knowing Your Life Goals, Work, Career, and Retirement Goals
　…Celebrating Friendships.
　…Celebrating Relationships.
　…Embracing Your Journey and Having Fun.
　…Knowing What Motivates You.
　…Revealing Your Inner Wisdom.
　…Discovering Your Creativity.
　…Increasing Your Confidence.
　…Recognizing Your Inner Beauty.
　…Discovering Your Inner Joy.
　…Recognizing Your Seasons of Change.

www.ingramcontent.com/pod-product-compliance
Lightning Source LLC
LaVergne TN
LVHW021738060526
838200LV00052B/3350